2nd Edition

Written By: W. R. Gittens

Design By: Script Lobby

Original Art By: W. Gittens & J. Joseph

Edited By: M. Gittens, C. Joseph & E. Gittens

This series of books is mostly based on true events and is dedicated to all parents who take the time to bond with their kids by spending time with them.

Today was Saturday, and Isaiah was excited. It was the first weekend of spring, and Isaiah was eager to help his dad do spring chores in the yard. He was happy that spring had arrived. He could hear the birds singing in the air, so he jumped out of bed and ran to his window.

The sun had started to peek out in the clear blue sky as he looked out the window. It was still early in the morning, and the trees had fresh new green leaves. He was so excited that today was sunny and bright, that he thought to himself; "what fun stuff can I do outside today?"

Suddenly he remembered that his dad was doing the annual *"BIG SPRING YARD CLEANUP"* today, and had promised him during winter, that he could help when the day arrived.

Excited, he ran downstairs into the kitchen to look for Dad, but it was quiet. "Mom and Dad are still asleep," he thought to himself, so he ran back upstairs and burst into their room yelling: "Wake up Dad I'm ready to work!"

Dad rolled over lazily and replied, "Isaiah, it's too early, and I must rest a bit longer."

"But Dad, it's the first day of spring and you promised I could help with the *BIG SPRING YARD CLEANUP* today!" Isaiah exclaimed.

"Sure Isaiah, I remember, but I need just a little more rest, so hurry along and I will be up in an hour." Dad said and went back to sleep.

"Ok!" Isaiah said and went off to play until Dad woke up.

"Hmmm, what can I do while I wait on Dad?" Isaiah thought to himself. He smiled. "I'll get dressed and play with my toys in the meantime." He put his favorite spring coat on and then played with his toys while he waited for Dad to get out of bed.

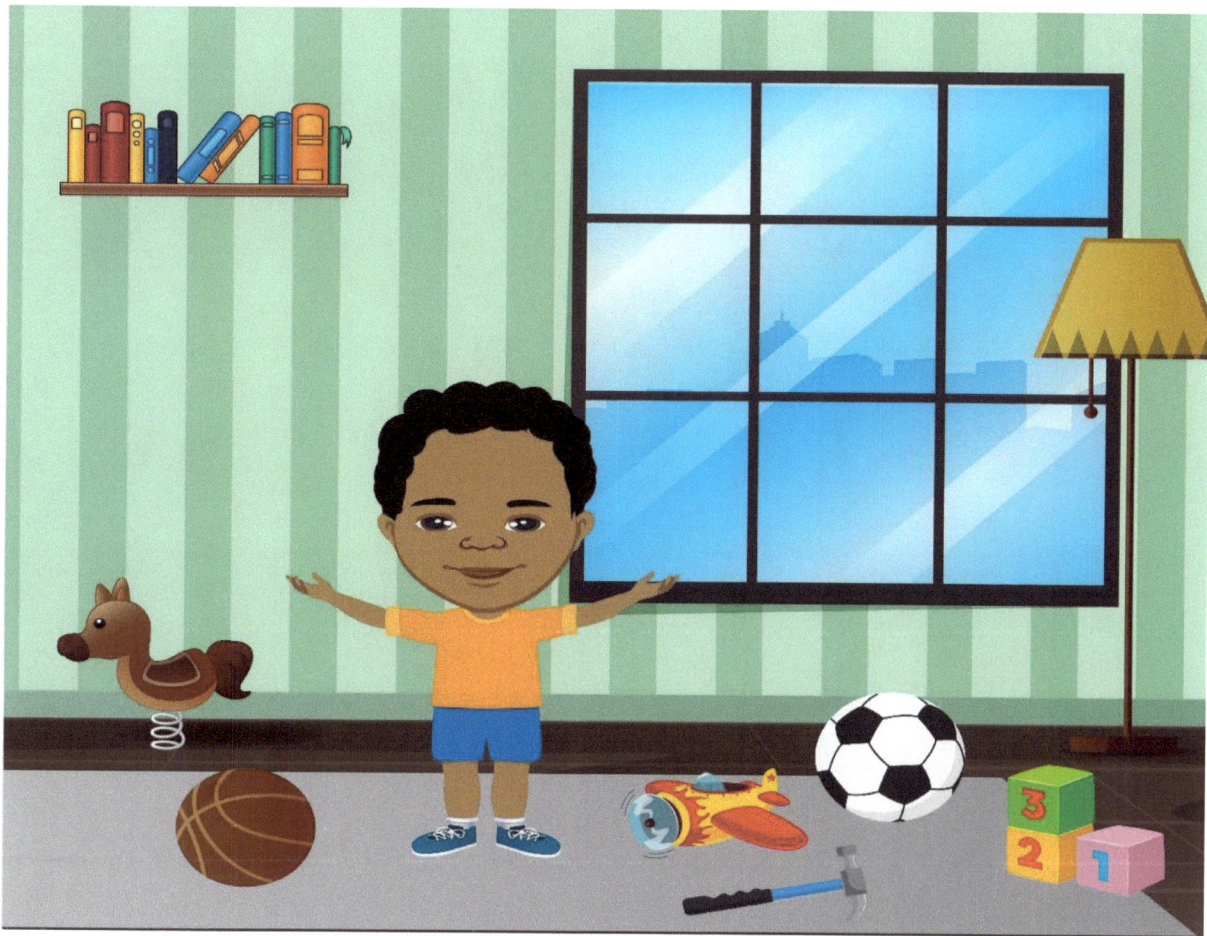

At last, Dad got up, and they went downstairs to have a marvelous breakfast of waffles and eggs.

After breakfast, it was off to get ready for spring cleanup and planting. Dad and Isaiah put on their boots and gloves and then they were ready to go. As Dad opened the door, Isaiah yelled: "Wait, Dad, I have to get my tool set."

Dad had bought him a new tool set for Christmas and he was eager to use it. His toy set had many wonderful tools, and Isaiah was sure that he could use them to help Dad rake the leaves, trim the shrubs or weeds, and plant many beautiful flowers in the yard.

"Yippee!" Isaiah smiled to himself and thought about how much fun it was going to be as he bent to pick up his tool box. He always enjoyed helping Dad do chores around the yard and he couldn't wait to begin exploring nature.

Suddenly, Dad gave the familiar call "Isaiah let's go!"

"I'm coming Dad!" Isaiah yelled excitedly as he picked up his tool set and ran out to meet him in the yard.

All winter long, he had been eating his fruits and vegetables to be healthy and strong to help with the spring cleanup, and now he was ready to show Dad how strong he was.

Dad and Isaiah walked to the toolshed where Dad kept his tools. Dad took out his shears to prune the shrubs, a rake to rake the leaves, a shovel to dig holes to plant the flowers, some trash bags to put the leaves, a wheelbarrow to move dirt, and a watering can to water the flowers.

Now they were ready to start. It was such a sunny spring day that they removed their coats before starting work. "What are we going to do first?" Isaiah asked. Once he had all of his tools, Dad said: "First we will trim the shrubs, then rake the leaves, and put it all in the trash bags. After that, we will pull the weeds from the garden, plant the flowers and water them to make them grow."

With a smile on his face, Isaiah opened his tool set and grabbed his shears, rake, and shovel, just like Dad did, then, they started cutting the shrubs. They chatted as they worked.

"Dad where do the birds go during winter and why are the bees flying around the flowers now?" Isaiah asked. Dad replied: "Some birds fly to warmer places when winter arrives and return when spring returns. It's a long journey, but they go every year to keep warm. The bees go into their hives to pass the winter and when spring arrives, they come out to visit the flowers to collect a sweet liquid called nectar.

Some bees use it for food, but honeybees use it to make honey which you love so much. When they touch the flowers, they pick up and drop off stuff called pollen which allows plants and flowers to keep blooming every year."

As Isaiah helped Dad cut the shrubs, he saw Matt the next door neighbor in his yard. "Hello Matt, what are you doing today?" they called out. "Hello Isaiah, I see you are helping Dad with the yard cleanup. I am about to do a big yard cleanup just like you are."

Suddenly Isaiah heard a loud sound. Matt had started his electric leaf blower. *Whirr, whirr, whirr* went the blower as Matt quickly blew the leaves and bagged them.

Next Matt started his grass trimmer. *Buzz, buzz, buzz*, went the trimmer as Matt quickly cut the weeds.

As the machines *whined*, *whirred*, and *buzzed*, loudly, Isaiah and Dad could no longer hear each other so they stopped talking. Matt quickly completed his yard cleanup and waved goodbye.

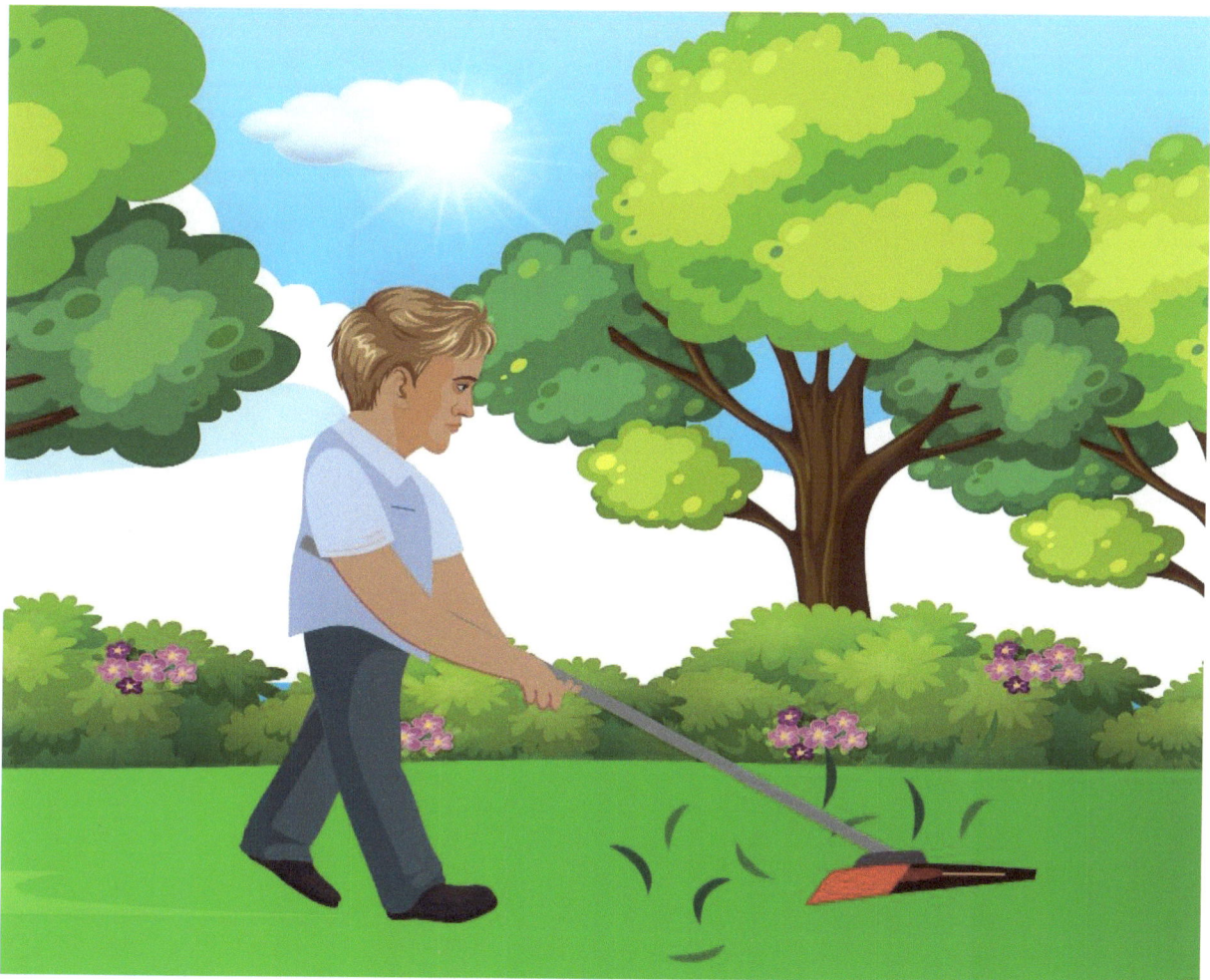

After they had pruned the shrubs, they raked the leaves.

Next, they pulled the weeds.

Then they planted the flowers in the garden that Dad had bought the night before from the local nursery. While Dad used his big shovel to make holes in the ground to plant the flowers, Isaiah also used his small shovel to make holes.

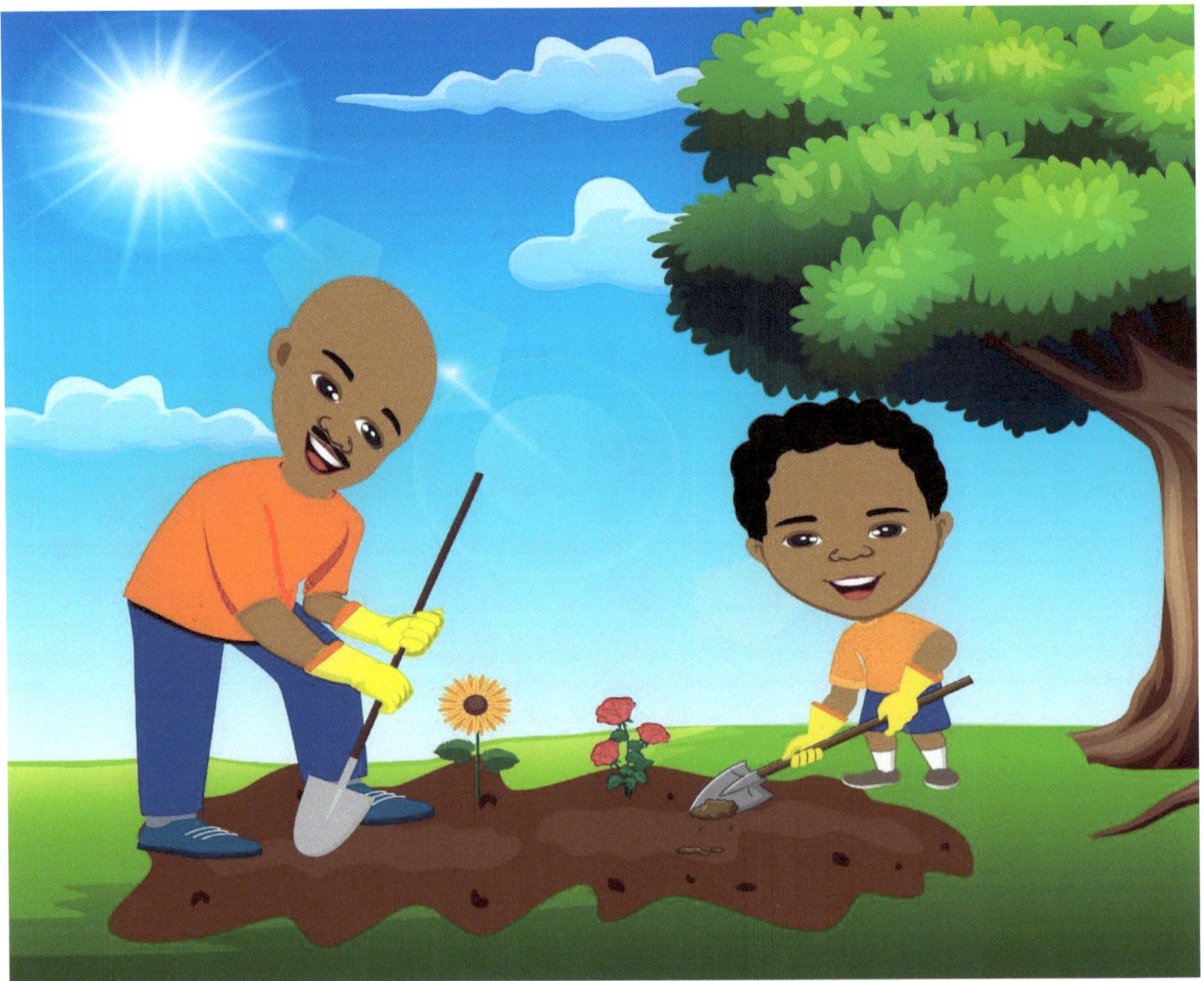

When they were finished planting the flowers, Isaiah curiously asked, "Dad, can I help water the flowers?" "Sure," Dad replied, and Isaiah ran off to fill his can with water. After he had watered the flowers, Isaiah exclaimed, "Oh, this was so much fun!"

Just as they were finished, Mom called them in for some refreshing lemonade. Isaiah and Dad were both thirsty, and Mom's lemonade tasted really good on such a hot spring day.

Later that evening, as Dad tucked Isaiah into bed, Isaiah thought about how much fun it had been helping Dad in the yard. Then with a smile on his face, Isaiah said: "Dad, Matt cleaned his yard super fast!! Why did we use a rake to rake the leaves and our hands to pull weeds?" Dad smiled and looked at Isaiah, as he continued to ask another question.

"Why don't you use the leaf blower and the grass trimmer like Matt did?"

Once again Dad looked at Isaiah and smiled. "If I had used the blower and trimmer, I would not be able to hear your questions and you would not be able to hear me telling you about all the interesting things we saw in the yard."

Isaiah looked at Dad with a smile and tiredly said: "Dad was I strong today?"

"You were Isaiah, and without your help, I would not have finished the cleanup today," Dad said.

As he drifted off to sleep, Isaiah responded: "Love you, Dad! I really enjoyed helping you and I can't wait for our next BIG YARD CLEANUP."

"Me too," Dad replied quietly, but Isaiah didn't hear, because he was already fast asleep.

THE END

Scan to visit the website to claim the "Early Bird" promotion gift.

www.ingramcontent.com/pod-product-compliance
Lightning Source LLC
Chambersburg PA
CBHW042128040426

42450CB00002B/110